Art for Healing®
Painting Your Heart Out

By Laurie Zagon, M.F.A.
Founder/Director, Art & Creativity for Healing, Inc.

ACKNOWLEDGMENTS

I would like to acknowledge my extraordinary husband Joe Sorrentino, for his continuous love and support for me and Art & Creativity for Healing. I could not have done it without him!

To all of the Art & Creativity for Healing Facilitators who carry the message on a daily basis to our partner agencies. We could not do it without you! Thank you to all the board members, staff, and donors who serve and support Art & Creativity for Healing.

A very special thank you to Genna Conrad, Stephanie Eberhard, Vicki Merrill, Laurie Miller, and Nancy Filson.

CONTENTS

FORWARD
By Dallas M. Stout

As the Managing Director of one of the largest residential facilities for troubled youth in Orange County, California, I received calls every week from great folks with wonderful programs for sale. Unfortunately, as is true with most nonprofit programs, our budgets were always tight and we could seldom afford these extra expenses. That is why I was not too enthused when one of my staff asked to talk to me one day about a friend of hers who was recommending a new healing art program for our youth. I was not as impressed by this program as my staff was—I was sure this free workshop would contain a 'hard sell' right after hooking the youth in the first class. After much discussion and several phone calls to check references, I reluctantly agreed to allow Art & Creativity for Healing to come in and do a class for a group of our youth.

The children we worked with at this agency were not always quick to accept to new 'educational' experiences. This was especially true of things that they had failed at in the past or that might not be seen as 'cool' on the streets. Thus, the first group of kids we put together to take the class were not necessarily excited to have been chosen for the experience. For the most part, the first group went because they knew it was a one-time thing.

Our experience with the Art & Creativity for Healing program was that it was an all-inclusive class. All we had to do was provide a room with tables and chairs and, of course, the children. The instructors brought high quality art supplies, plastic to keep paint off of the tables and floors, special music, and lots of smiles and hugs. The youth came away from the class with small canvas boards that they had painted and a new appreciation for art. I was not aware of any child who had had a bad experience or felt like they couldn't paint (which was the number one fear going in) after taking the class. The youth in that first class must have made quite an impression on the Art & Creativity for Healing instructors because much more good came out of it.

Shortly after providing initial classes for a couple groups of our kids, Laurie Zagon contacted me and began discussing the possibility of putting together a series of art classes. I was more interested at this point due to the rave reviews from workshop participants who were proud of their artwork. The decision was made to move ahead with a four-week class that would focus on a different genre of art each week. Shortly after the second class of this four-week series, I happened to walk into our conference room where the classes were being held. In the corner were piles of artwork in frames stacked neatly on a table. Later that day, I asked the children about it and they responded that it was their artwork from the classes. Not only had Art & Creativity for Healing provided us with all the art supplies for the classes, but they also provided frames in which to hang the completed works of art. Walking back into my business trailer it dawned on me how nice it might be to hang some of the artwork in the facility. Without asking or telling the youth what we were doing, we took the artwork and set about decorating the walls of the facility.

Almost overnight there was an explosion of colorful, resident-created artwork adorning the walls of the facility. The staff and I noticed right away how much attention and excitement the artwork was generating amongst our residents. I couldn't walk from one place to another without being stopped by a proud resident who wanted me to know that their artwork was on the walls. The residents showed me aspects of their work and told me how it was related to their experiences and troubles. They spoke of shadows and darkness turning into forgiveness and hope—all in the colors on the canvas— and explained why they had done things certain ways. Facility tours provided to guests by the youth always came to a halt in front of their artwork as they described their journeys through the colors on our walls. Together, we had started something very meaningful to these children and their families, as well as to our guests and staff team.

As soon as the first four-week series was complete, our youth were asking for more classes. We started the first series again for a second group of youth and involved some from the first class as 'helpers'. These residents proudly wore the Art & Creativity for Healing apron they were given by the adult volunteers. This fit perfectly with our treatment philosophy that involved kids who had been in the program longer in helping the newer residents.

There is considerable research that shows that youth helping youth builds assets for everyone involved. The positive energy coming from our youth at this point made it easy for Laurie to create a second, slightly more advanced four-week series for our residents who had completed the first series. Soon we had multiple Art & Creativity for Healing classes going on. The teachers began to ask what was going on, as some of the artwork was making its way back into the school classrooms—these works of art were being integrated into school assignments by our resourceful residents.

Later, even more components were designed and implemented with much success. An anger management module was added after one of the Art & Creativity for Healing volunteers commented about the amount of black and red paint being used in the workshops. This observation made perfect sense to me due to the traumatic experiences that our youth had often experienced prior to their arrival. I went out of my way to encourage the kids to expand their color palettes. Even so, there was a small minority of youth who never painted with anything other than black and red. Most started out that way and painted with more light and color as they felt better about the work and ultimately themselves.

As children completed the residential portion of our treatment and moved back home as 'live outs', they continued to talk about the art classes. If they happened to be visiting in the facility when the volunteers arrived for classes, they always ran to participate and express continued interest in the program. Again I was contacted by Laurie to see how I felt about another series of art classes for the 'live outs'. I was interested; however we just didn't have the space in our facility to support any more classes. Ever resourceful, Laurie arranged for me and one of my staff to meet with herself and a local hotel manager to consider holding the classes there. After working out the details, several of these classes were held for the 'live outs' and their parents at the hotel.

About twice a year, we held a very intensive psychodrama and therapy experience for a small group of residents. These life changing experiences called marathons generally lasted 24 to 30 hours and took months of preparation to get the group ready. The intensives were designed to allow the residents to let go of their pasts, and generally were a highly emotional experience for everyone involved. I approached Laurie after one such marathon, and asked her if we could make an Art & Creativity for Healing class coincide with the follow-up process. Soon residents were painting about their marathon experiences as well.

After the implementation of this program, there was no one in the facility more impressed than I by what had transpired through our partnership with Art & Creativity for Healing. From my vantage point at the helm, I could clearly see that much more was happening than just a series of art classes. What I saw was no less than a major transformation of our program. Our youth, who began the program grumbling about how 'lame' painting was and that they were not going to do it, suddenly were begging for more classes at every opportunity. It was no secret that I was a huge fan of Art & Creativity for Healing at this point. I wrote letters of support for their funders, and for their newsletters. I appeared in their fundraising videos and I was the keynote speaker at their first "Palette of Colors" fundraising dinner. I even sold their Christmas cards to ensure their continued operation in our program.

Not only were our kids leaving the workshops with an increased confidence in their artistic abilities, they were leaving the workshops with an increased sense of an overall 'can do' attitude. This attitude change and increase in personal confidence on the part of our residents impacted all levels of our program. Soon, residents were applying themselves and working harder in math or English class because they had 'conquered' art class. They held their heads a little higher as they fulfilled their leadership responsibilities around the facility. They spoke of learning more about themselves as a result of the art classes when they went into the community to do speaking engagements. In addition to all of these wonderful changes, we also had a much more beautiful, brightly colored and engaging facility.

I'm not sure I could find the words to fully express what really happened in our facility—we really don't need words to articulate what we saw unfold before our very eyes. Even now, years later, I am contacted by youth who went through those classes and are still talking about it. Plainly said, Art & Creativity for Healing classes change lives! You have a brush in your hand and you're applying colors to a canvas.

Laurie Zagon

At the same time, you are releasing and expressing emotions, and getting in touch with feelings that were perhaps long overdue to come to the surface. That was certainly the case with my kids in this program.

Dallas M. Stout, Psy.D.
Doctors Nonprofit Consulting
Fullerton, California

"We need to give each other the space to grow, to be ourselves, to exercise our diversity. We need to give each other space so that we may both give and receive such beautiful things as ideas, openness, dignity, joy, healing, and inclusion."

- Unknown

"Just as despair can come to one only from other human beings, hope, too, can be given to one only by other human beings."

- Elie Weisel

INTRODUCTION

It is with great joy that I introduce all of you to this work. I feel extremely blessed to be an artist and equally blessed to be a teacher. I have always known that the creative process is open for everyone to utilize and that the potential for being an artist is inherent in every human being. I believe that God is the Master Creator. He has taught us that we too can create things that have never been seen before using color and painting as a vessel for expression. The Master Creator has shown us that a blank canvas represents a new start. Something fresh and new can always be born through paint and a blank canvas. The first stroke of color that penetrates the white canvas signals the start of a very exciting period that continues through the beginning, middle, and end of the work of art. I personally have always felt an amazing surge of energy when I complete a painting. The energy of that completion often propels me to begin the next piece.

As a teacher and professor of art for over 30 years I have personally instructed over 15,000 students in the Art for Healing process. Every human being has his or her own personal art stroke! Just like a person's handwriting, the art stroke represents that individual's unique touch when applying an abstract color on canvas or paper. I have seen children, teens, and adults transcend before my eyes, especially the ones who insist they cannot draw a straight line, but joined the class despite their presumed inadequacies. They are the ones who always create the most outstanding pieces in the class. I love their faces when they see their completed work of art displayed in the front of the room, and when another student comments on how much they love that particular painting.

Many adults stop creating art after childhood because they had a grade school teacher who told them their work was wrong because it did not look like the sample shown, or perhaps these adults have someone in the family who claimed the title of artist, and they feel as if they cannot compete with that person.

I am often disappointed with educators who show an example of what the art should look like, and ask pupils to imitate what is there in front of them. Many kids become frustrated and feel as if they fail as an artist if they cannot imitate the example in front of them.

I encourage educators to offer students a way to express their uniqueness. Turn on some music and let them abstractly interpret with colors based on what they hear. You will be amazed at how effective this method can be. Let your students first find their own creative voice by looking inside instead of outside. I facilitate workshops for children 6 years and up. All of them enjoy our method and ask when they can come back for more.

The methods I developed began in the mid-eighties in New York City, after spending 14 years as a university professor of art. As much as I loved teaching painting, design, and color, I began to see something missing in the fine arts curriculum. This became even clearer as I observed my students. Because there was such an increasing emphasis on technique, many of them failed to find their own voice as artists. I began experimenting with a few assignments that encouraged the students to look inside for their ideas by painting to instrumental jazz. I would begin by asking them to close their eyes, take a deep breath, and relax.

With a palette of Red, Yellow, Blue, Orange, Green and Violet, Black, White and Brown, they would intuitively select and mix colors inspired by the music. Within minutes I could see their hands dancing across the canvases. Initially, I created a 30-45 minute period for them to complete the work of art. The students were amazed at the results. The dialogue went on for an additional hour or so. The students were on fire over this simple little exercise. They wanted to do more. I continued to give them more, and encouraged them to create a series of twelve works of art using a personal theme that reflected something important going on in their lives.

Some chose family/health issues, others chose romantic relationships, and a few chose to work intuitively without a specific theme. Again and again, the results were unique and authentic works of art that the students felt were coming from a place inside themselves that they had never expressed before.

I share my story in hopes that anyone reading it will realize there are many ways for people to open up creatively. I also hope that anyone who has a vision for something they feel passionate about will be inspired by the story of how Art & Creativity for Healing began, and take that leap of faith! There will be failure before success, but if you pray about it every day, you will become of service to others and reap the rewards of success as you find new direction in your life.

I truly believe that all human beings are wired for creativity. Opening the creative center can happen by painting a painting, writing a poem, planting a garden, cooking, jewelry making, sewing, et cetera. Once that creative center is open, just dust out those cobwebs, and see how invigorating your life becomes.

In addition to my own story, included in this book are eight inspirational vignettes from students who have benefited from the Art & Creativity for Healing work.

Laurie Zagon, Founder/Director
Art & Creativity for Healing, Inc.

PART ONE
The History and Origin of Art & Creativity for Healing

I was born and raised in Queens, New York, in an Archie Bunker-style row house that was attached to the neighbors on both sides. There were three floors to this home. The top floor had three bedrooms and a bathroom; the ground level had a living room, dining room, and kitchen with a small powder room; the bottom floor was the basement, which served a double purpose as my art studio—and my mom's laundry room. The size of the space was approximately 300 square feet. I spent most of my childhood in that basement. It was my special place to create many works of art.

My parents did not get along very well and there was always a lot of screaming and yelling upstairs, which was one of the reasons I spent so much time in the basement—it was my safe place. I loved being alone in that little basement and escaping into my own little world of art. I would draw, paint, create collages, et cetera, but my favorite was always oil painting. Of course, that was my mother's least favorite due to the smell of linseed oil and turpentine. She was also quite nervous about me getting paint on the clothes that were hanging on the clothesline right down the middle of my 'atelier'. I did my best not to make a mess.

I believe my interest in art began around the age of five. In school I had wonderful teachers who encouraged me to develop my artistic talent. By the time I reached Junior High I was fortunate enough to have the best art teacher at the school. Her name was Mrs. Polansky. She was talented and beautiful. I learned so much from her—drawing, painting, printmaking, and sculpture. I wanted to learn more, and one day a fellow student told me that the highly acclaimed High School of Art & Design was accepting applications from students all over the city. I applied and was thrilled to be accepted in the fall of 1965. That was truly the beginning of being surrounded by great young artists. Many of the artists were more talented than I was. At first I felt extremely inadequate, but soon the abundance of talent made me want to work even harder. I graduated in 1968 with a major in painting along with a large body of work. This gave me the opportunity to apply to an art college where I would ultimately receive my Bachelor's Degree in Fine Art (B.F.A). I was accepted at the Maryland Institute College of Art in Baltimore, Maryland, where I was once again surrounded by talented students, and by Professors who were highly acclaimed artists themselves.

At the Maryland Institute College of Art, my work flourished and I began entering shows and selling my work, which confirmed to me that this was what I was born to do. When I paint I go to an inspired place that transcends my everyday life. For me it has always been a spiritual experience; painting establishes a connection that makes me feel like an open vessel being filled with warmth and comfort.

In 1971, I was accepted to Syracuse University as a graduate student with a full fellowship to study art. It was there that my work took on a new direction. I spent two glorious years producing a large body of work that consisted of over thirty 6' x 7' foot canvases. I also taught foundation classes to freshman students in order to fulfill my fellowship requirements. That is where I fell in love with teaching.

It was such a joy to teach students who were in the same age group as myself. I enjoyed bringing out the best in them through art. Not only could I pass on the gift of art, but I could see a passion igniting in beginner artists. I completed my M.F.A in 1973 and moved back to New York City to continue my career as an artist and teacher. I found a great studio space, and I was fortunate to be hired by the City University of New York (CUNY) at Queens College as a part-time professor of art.

My experiences at Syracuse University teaching color theory and basic design helped me to become an attractive candidate for the art department at Queens College. My career flourished in New York, and I began selling a lot of paintings to both individuals and corporations. Teaching kept me grounded and humble by enabling me to serve as a mentor to my students. I discovered that I was good at helping people realize their potential as artists, and with finding their unique artistic voice.

One of my favorite experiences during my 14 years at Queens College was my interaction with students. Nothing gave me more pleasure than to help my students become inspired by art. It was extremely rewarding to have students tell me that my encouragement gave them the strength they needed to pursue advanced work in color and painting. But as I continued teaching basic and fundamental fine arts classes, I began to feel that something was missing in my teaching—I needed to find a way for students to discover their own uniqueness as artists. I found that there was often a lack of soul in the students' work because they were so busy trying to perfect a specific technique.

During my teaching career, I had the opportunity to take "Technologies for Creating" with Robert Fritz who is an acclaimed author, musician, and educator. He created seminars for people to learn more about using the creative process in their daily lives. The seminar I attended was a 5-week course with one of his trained seminar leaders, which was a great influence on me as an artist and teacher in that it gave me insight into the structure of creativity. I began to take chances and risks with my own work like I had never done before.

I had always been a painter, but greatly admired sculptors. I wanted to create some large-scale sculptures but felt intimidated. After taking a few of the seminars, and then becoming one of the instructors, I created an entire collection of three-dimensional paintings. I created 3-panel screens as well as giant arches for people to walk through. I recommend that everyone read Robert Fritz's books, "The Path of Least Resistance" and "Your Life as Art".

During that time, I also created my first "Color & Play for the Inner Child" workshop for stressed out Wall Street executives. These seminars were 3 hours long and enabled participants to express themselves using paint and color abstractly on canvas. Most of the workshop participants had not painted since they were in kindergarten. They loved having the opportunity to do something that was so entirely different from their regular everyday lives. They were miraculously transformed during the workshops, discovering the creativity of their inner child.

These workshops were successful and I continued to receive referrals from my Wall Street students. The success of these workshops lead to continued referrals, bringing stock brokers, bankers, lawyers, and other professionals to participate in them over the course of two years. In 1989, I relocated from New York City to Southern California, where I met my husband Joe Sorrentino, also known as "Rainbow Joe". Joe received this nickname from the children who participated in my workshops for children with HIV/AIDS at Children's Hospital of Los Angeles in 1990—they loved his rainbow suspenders that he wore when he visited them.

Shortly after, I met the acclaimed author and psychologist Claudia Black, who is best known for her books about addiction and alcoholism. I had previously met with Claudia's editor from Ballantine/Random House Books to discuss how some of my paintings could be used as illustrations in a new book by Claudia entitled *"It's Never Too Late To Have a Happy Childhood: Inspirations for Inner Healing"*. That was the beginning of a great collaboration that introduced me to many of Claudia's colleagues, including marriage and family therapists, and social workers in the South Orange County region of Southern California. After the book came out, I was asked to facilitate "Color & Play for the Inner Child" workshops similar to the ones I had done in New York.

The first workshop was at a local treatment center for recovering alcoholics that focused on recovery from addiction. I worked closely with a therapist who specialized in this area to create assignments for 15 participants. I also developed questions that they could answer by painting colors on canvas. This workshop was a success, which lead to requests for more specialized group workshops. There were cardiac patient groups, cancer support groups, children and adults with HIV/AIDS, teen substance abuse groups, et cetera. I received no compensation for this, and while I did need to make a living, somehow I had become addicted to serving others—I didn't really see this as a means of support but rather as a new way of life. Many friends knew of my volunteer projects and either came along to help out, or stuffed a $20 bill in my pocket and said, "Here—go buy some art supplies to help those people you work with." I continued the workshops in Southern California until 1994, when my husband Joe was transferred to Flagstaff, Arizona.

In Flagstaff, I immediately became involved with Big Brothers/Big Sisters of Northern Arizona. I was a Big Sister to a young disabled teen named Tina. Tina loved art and she and I spent most Saturdays hanging out and painting together. Kay, the Director of the agency,

Laurie Zagon

asked me to do several workshops for that program. I also became involved with the local cancer center and the local AIDS Services Center. It was a wonderful time for me to write new curriculum and concentrate on creating new works of art. For example, I co-authored with Sara Marberry "The Power of Color: Creating Healthy Interior Spaces". I was also invited to present continuing education unit workshops through the local American Society of Interior Designers (ASID) throughout many cities in the U.S. This provided an earned income that helped me support the free workshops.

In 1994, Joe and I moved back to California and settled in to a live/work art studio in Los Angeles at the Brewery Arts Colony. It was there that I reconnected with other artists and further expanded my interest in working with nonprofits—I did this by helping the 500+ artists who showed their work at the twice yearly art walks become a nonprofit public benefit art association. I became actively involved in helping local charities have a presence at our art walks. This brought in many new groups of people who ultimately bought art directly from the artists during the open studio art walks. The involvement with the local L.A. charities is what ultimately birthed my interest in wanting to start a nonprofit.

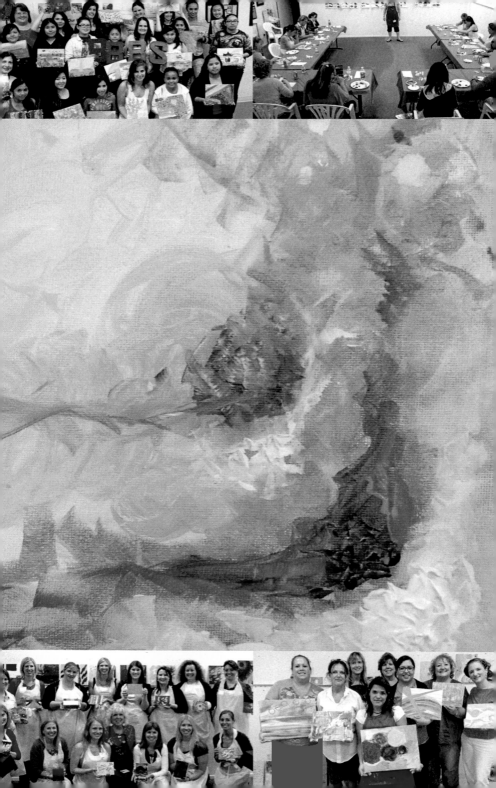

PART TWO
The Process—Why Our Workshops Attract Participants

Tens of thousands of individuals have benefited from the "Art for Healing" process because there is no previous art experience required—anyone can do it. The abstract nature of our methods has been proven to be successful in removing the anxiety or fear of not knowing how to draw something representational, which many people experience when signing up for an art class.

Individuals suffering from abuse, illness, grief, and stress are attracted to our programs because the language of color and painting on canvas enables them to say things they have no words for, but can express with dabs of color.

I created the "Art for Healing" process back in 1987 when I started an art workshop for stressed out Wall Street executives. The program was based on a series of questions that I asked and they answered abstractly with color. I found that this method of painting using non-representational abstractions was highly effective in getting these executives to be honest about what was truly going on in their lives. Workshop participants felt safe and comfortable enough to express themselves when I explained that due to the abstract nature of the art, no one, with the exception of themselves, would ever really know what the painting was about. I knew I was onto something special when many of them not only wanted to repeat the class but also wanted to invite their friends and family. I had accomplished what I had set out to do—helping people become excited about the creative process, while feeling comfortable enough to create acrylic paintings in short periods of time.

I continued to develop and refine the "Art for Healing" process after relocating to California in 1989. I initially joined forces with a few great Marriage & Family Therapists and Social Workers. With their input, I developed a series of questions for my "Color & Play for the Inner Child" workshops. These clinicians were extremely insightful and helpful in assisting me with ideas on how to create a specific curriculum for their clients who were suffering from issues related to abuse, addiction, illness, grief, and stress. From the beginning, I made it clear that I was approaching as an artist, not a therapist. I have great respect for the profession of art therapy, and it is a profession that requires a university degree. What is different about Art & Creativity for Healing is that while we encourage participants to talk about their own work if they choose to, we never comment on or analyze their work. We also encourage each of our participants to take their completed works of art to show and discuss with their therapist, counselor, or social worker.

Over the years, I have had many opportunities that enabled me to develop specific curriculums for specific needs. In 1991, I was given the extraordinary opportunity to collaborate with social workers who specialized in working with children with HIV/AIDS at Children's Hospital of Los Angeles (CHLA). One of the staff members was very specific in what she wanted me to achieve with 5-14 year olds with full blown AIDS. At first I was taken aback by what she wanted me to have them process with colors. The title of the painting was; "A Look Inside My Body: The Colors of How I Feel About Being Sick".

The following is a list of questions that I developed for her program:

Express with 2 colors for 2 minutes (The reason for the short interval of time is so they do not spend time overthinking the exercise. The spontaneity helps dissipate anxiety about doing it right):

1. The feeling of being sick
2. Feeling too sick to play
3. The feeling of coming to the hospital
4. The feeling of having tests done at the hospital
5. Feeling scared
6. Feeling afraid of never getting well again
7. Feeling scared of dying
8. The feeling of holding God's hand
9. The feeling of how much fun it is to paint this painting

I told the therapist that I wasn't sure I could do this without crying. She looked at me with stern eyes, got right in my face and said, "This is not about you, this is about them having a professional like you facilitate an Art for Healing workshop. There are many people here that can cry with them and pray with them, but we do not have anyone that can do what you do." I felt like I got slapped across the face a few times. It was sobering! To this day I think back about how that was the greatest lesson I could ever have learned about my role as an Art for Healing facilitator.

At CHLA, we worked on 16" x 20" canvases, so it took about 30 minutes to complete the paintings. There were fifteen children ages 5-14. We also had a few healthy siblings that processed the painting by expressing what they were feeling about their brother or sister having AIDS. I was apprehensive about how the sharing would go, but to my surprise all of the children wanted to talk about what they had done in their paintings. It was hard at moments to hold back the tears, but I knew I was there to be a facilitator and not there to cry for them as the counselor had pointed out to me before the workshop.

One after another all 14 kids shared. It took about an hour and a half, which gave me more insight on how important it is to allow enough time for sharing. The kids needed to process what they had done— that takes time if each child needs 5-10 minutes to go through the list of questions with the facilitator. The children and their families were pleased with the workshops and I was invited back to facilitate more over time. I even created a traveling exhibit with the paintings from that very first workshop. We had photos of the kids painting along with their artwork. The show traveled to Arizona and several cities on the East Coast as part of an Arizona Arts Commission project.

Word got around, and I was invited to facilitate workshops for cancer patients and their families at City of Hope National Cancer Center. Nellie Garcia, the Director of Clinical Social Work, and I collaborated on a curriculum. Ms. Garcia had very specific ideas that she wanted me to include in my curriculum. Here is an example of the questions from the "Living with Cancer" workshop.

1. What were your feelings when you came to the hospital for tests?
2. What feelings did you have when you first heard the news about your cancer from your physician?
3. What did it feel like telling family and friends?
4. What did it feel like coming for treatments?

5. How do you feel right now?
6. How do you feel spiritually, about God?
7. Express your feelings of love—giving, receiving, or both.

My first workshop at City of Hope had 15 cancer patients and family members. The workshop was scheduled from 9 am-12 noon. I barely finished by noon because there was so much sharing. People seemed to open up like never before according to Ms. Garcia. Here is a quote about the workshops from her:

"Many of the patients and family members attending the Art for Healing workshops had been previously involved with other forms of therapy at City of Hope that had been unsuccessful. After attending one of these workshops, these same patients and family members experienced obvious breakthroughs in the process of their emotional healing. The families need a way to express the devastation they experience when someone in their family is stricken with a life-threatening illness. Art for Healing has given them a new way to communicate their feelings."

I continued for seven years to facilitate Art for Healing workshops at City of Hope. I trained facilitators and volunteers to join me. There were over 500 people who benefitted from our workshops.

When people ask me how I developed my curriculum, this is how it all got started. I have always worked with licensed clinicians at all of the hospitals, treatment centers, and nonprofit agencies. I have found them to be very helpful in guiding me on how to best tailor the workshop questions to each specific audience.

PART THREE
Lessons Learned—Starting a NonProfit

In 1996 my husband and I moved from Arizona back to Southern California. The company my husband worked for moved us there and back within a two year period. We loved our time in Flagstaff but were glad to return to sea level. After years of living in New York, going to museums and galleries, and having my own studio in the middle of Manhattan, I felt it was time for me to live and work around other artists again.

We had the opportunity to rent a 2000 square foot studio and residence in the Brewery Artist Colony in downtown Los Angeles. This is a fantastic community of over 500 artists living and working in the old Pabst Blue Ribbon Brewery. In the center of the Brewery property is a café where many of the artists in residence would come together for breakfast and lunch. It was there that I met a few of the artists who ran the twice yearly ARTWALK. This major event held over a weekend in the spring and fall invites 10,000+ visitors to tour the facility and visit many of the artist's studios. The visitors have a great opportunity to buy works of art directly from the artists, as well as visit the studios and meet the artists.

In 1996, when I joined the board of the Artwalk Association, it was primarily a group of artists getting together for a loosely structured evening of beer and arguments on how to organize the Artwalk events. A few of us took control and worked with an accountant who helped us apply to become a nonprofit association. This gave us the ability to receive sponsorships and underwriting for the Artwalk events. As one of the leaders, I began to engage other charities as partners in our events. Our very first partnership was with El Nido Family Centers. El Nido brought in their board members for a silent auction that we held, which helped them raise money for their charity and brought in supporters who purchased many works of art directly from the artists. This was a win-win for all. Over the next few years, our Artwalks grew larger than ever and many people came because of the partnerships with other charities.

During this time, I was also teaching part-time at Azusa Pacific University. I taught classes in Painting, Drawing, and Introduction to Art. The Chair of the Art Department allowed me to create a special class called City of Hope: Expressing Feelings with Color. The students would take a class with me two mornings a week, during which I would teach them to express what was going on in their lives using the Art for Healing methods I had begun during the 1980s in New York.

The students would then join me on three Saturday mornings at City of Hope National Cancer Center during which I would facilitate a three hour Art for Healing workshop for cancer patients and their families. This gave the students an opportunity to volunteer their time helping families stricken with life-threatening diseases. We had a wonderful response from the hospital patients and their families.

In 1999, I met a group of people who wanted to start a not-for-profit art school in South Orange County, California. Within a few months I joined the group, thinking that this was the perfect venue for my Art for Healing work. We opened and closed the school in less than a year. It was a very traumatic experience, but over time it has become one of the greatest gifts ever given to me.

There were five board members and two Executive Directors. The other director was an accomplished teacher/pianist and was passionate about teaching piano and voice. I, on the other hand, was interested in teaching Art for Healing classes and workshops. We hired a few part-time teachers to help us. I brought two of my favorite students from Azusa Pacific University to work with us—one to help out with administration, and the other to teach the children's basic art classes.

To explain what went wrong is easy in retrospect – two Executive Directors rather than one! My vision as one of the Executive Directors was to partner with other agencies in Orange County and Los Angeles by bringing Art for Healing classes to them. The other Executive Director purchased ten expensive pianos and proceeded to form a more traditional school for the arts, teaching piano and voice.

After operating for 5 months, the other director and the board members asked me to leave. They felt the other woman was a better fit for the school since she had invested thousands of dollars by purchasing the pianos. I, on the other hand, had worked 80-hour weeks without any remuneration, but did not put any cash into the organization. I could understand their point of view, but I was still very hurt. I felt like I had failed.

I went back to my nearby art studio and fell on my knees and cried. Totally defeated and alone, I let loose by crying out loud and asking God, "What did I do wrong? I thought you wanted me to be of service to others by teaching!" A booming voice—which, by the way, no one else could hear—said, "ART FOR HEALING STUPID!" I bolted upright, not believing what I heard. I felt it was God speaking to me. I also knew that God wouldn't call me stupid—it was my own critical inner voice. But then the booming voice spoke again and said, "START IT ALONE AND IT WILL BE BLESSED!"

I immediately got off my knees and ran to the phone to call my husband to tell him what had happened, and was very surprised at his response. I thought for sure he would tell me I was losing my mind. He said, "That is definitely a message from above. Go and start it and I will pay rent for the first year."

With his encouragement, I phoned the accountant who had helped me twice before in establishing the nonprofit artists association at the Brewery Artist Colony, and at the art school. My accountant, on the other hand, was not as receptive to the idea of me starting this new nonprofit. In fact his response was, "Are you crazy? After everything you have gone through, you want to go and do it again?"

I did manage to convince him, and within a week he prepared a new IRS application for me to start Art & Creativity for Healing, Inc., a nonprofit public benefit corporation. I sent in the application to the IRS knowing that it would take at least six months to a year to receive tax-exempt status. A week later I received a call from a woman representing the IRS. She introduced herself and proceeded to ask me a few questions. I held my breath for a few seconds before answering. Her main question concerned how many board members I had. The State of California requires at least three, but I already had this covered. I then asked, "How long will this process take?" She answered me with, "How long do you need it to take?" I explained to her that I would be eligible for foundation grants if I had the 501c3. She responded with, "Let me talk to my boss. Maybe we can fast-track it for you." I almost fell off my chair. The IRS saying they might fast-track my application was more than I could ever have hoped for. The next day I received a call back from the same woman and she informed me that my application was already approved and would be confirmed within the week. That is the moment that I truly knew that what I had heard that day in my studio was real—God had already begun blessing the Art for Healing work.

That first year we facilitated workshops for 1,000 children and adults suffering from abuse, illness, grief, and stress on-site at hospitals and other nonprofits. Our budget for the first year was $34,000. There was no money for salaries. My husband paid the rent, and I paid a few people to help with bookkeeping and administration. Most of the money that came in was from a grant from the Junior League of Orange County that enabled us to facilitate programs at the Boys and Girls Clubs of Garden Grove and Capistrano Valley. The rest of the funds were individual donations of $25-$100 from generous friends who believed in me and the Art & Creativity for Healing mission.

The second year we worked with 2,000 children and adults and our annual budget was $63,000. Word traveled fast—more people had heard about us and we had established an excellent reputation.

I recognized rather quickly that I had to bring in earned income rather than relying on grants from foundations. I decided to develop a training program for anyone wanting to learn our Art for Healing methods. I knew that artists, therapists, and educators would be interested in taking a two-day training that would give them a comprehensive training manual with assignments they could use in their practice. In addition, this training would provide them with Community Education and Professional Development credits needed for their annual Board of Behavioral Sciences CE/PD units in order to receive salary increases.

In 2001, I met a woman in my community who wanted to volunteer for our organization. She worked with me over a two-month period organizing all of my assignments and creating a format for the manual.

One of my board members took all of this work and formatted it on the computer, creating the first edition of the Level One Art for Healing Facilitator Training Manual. I spoke about the upcoming training at all of our workshops as well as circulated a brochure. It was also featured on our website.

We had 15 trainees sign up and pay $395 for our very first training in July of 2001. To date, we have graduated more than 500 people from our Level One Art for Healing Facilitator Training. In 2002, we began offering a Level Two Art for Healing Facilitator Training, and have awarded Brandman University Art for Healing Certifications to over 200 participants, many of whom have become certified in this process and now teach for us at the 35 sites we serve throughout Orange County, California.

Due to the enormous success of our 2-day training programs, we were approached in 2005 by Chapman University Extended Education in Orange, California, to create the first Art for Healing Certificate Program. To date we have graduated hundreds of extraordinary students who are now teaching our process in their communities. Chapman University offers the Certificate Program four times a year, including a 7-Day Summer Intensive for anyone around the country (or world) who would like to learn our methods in an accelerated learning program.

All of the above trainings have created a cash flow of income to help Art & Creativity for Healing pay its overhead costs. That has given us the flexibility to use 100% of all donations for programs. Much of our success was due to the amazing wisdom and experience of the people who volunteered to help and to guide us.

Best Practices for Starting a Nonprofit
- Pray for guidance
- Memorize and live your mission
- Do not get DISCOURAGED!
- Move forward and take action steps everyday
- Surround yourself with professional people
- Tell everyone you know what you are doing
- Be passionate when telling your story
- Stay humble & grateful by realizing you have been given a gift

PART FOUR
Testimonials

MARY BETH'S STORY

My family and I moved to Southern California in August 2003. After struggling financially for many years in our hometown, we decided to make a fresh start. We wanted a new life in a warm, sunny climate. My husband of 20 years had arrived 4 months earlier to start a new job. I stayed back to let our daughter finish the school year and to sell our home. I continued to work as long as possible while packing up our lives.

Upon our arrival, my focus was to handle all the things that go along with relocation. I unpacked our belongings, tried to find my way around, found new doctors, enrolled my daughter in school, found a daycare for my son, looked for a new job for myself, and tried to organize our very unsettled lives. It took about 3 or 4 months to get settled. After I started back to work and some sort of normalcy began to set in, the emotions that I had had no time to process for over a year started to rear their ugly head.

Did we do the right thing? I began to cry often. I missed the "familiar"— even the bad familiar. I had been an "East Coast girl" for 42 years and now I was on the West Coast. I felt like I was in a different country some of the time. I had been an interior designer for more than 20 years and even that felt different. Design terms that we used on the East Coast didn't translate on the West Coast. I began to question everything.

One day while reading a local magazine I saw an article featuring Art & Creativity for Healing. I had been looking for something like what I was reading about for a long time. There was nothing like this organization where I came from. I phoned Art & Creativity for Healing and Laurie answered. I recognized the accent right away. I grew up and lived in upstate New York, but I went to design school in New York City. Laurie felt like a bit of home—the familiarity that I had been lacking. Laurie explained her background and the organization, and in March of 2004 I took my first workshop.

"Expressing Feelings with Color" on a Sunday afternoon was my introduction to the amazing process. Today I am a firm believer in the positive impact that the process has on an individual struggling to overcome emotional issues such as the ones I was facing.

Growing up, I had always had the arts in my life. I took dancing from the age of 3, and played the flute for many years. My mother wanted to be an art teacher but the art supplies and art school were too expensive, so she chose elementary education. She was a very creative person and was living her dream through the creative endeavors of her children. At my elementary school in the late 60's, a new art teacher was hired. She was just out of college and wore clogs and wildly colorful clothes. My new art teacher exposed me and my creativity to various forms of art. I can still clearly remember some of the projects that we created—a watercolor painting of bugs, a tempera painting, weavings, and a "found objects" collage. We did coil clay pots thrown on the wheel. I loved to see how the glazes turned out.

It was at that same time that my home life began to get progressively worse. My father was an alcoholic. I was the youngest of 5 children, with my oldest sibling being 12 years older than me. As the older siblings started to go off to college, the dynamics of our home changed. As I got older, the problems were becoming more apparent to me. When I became a victim of sibling incest, the secrets began. I believe that if I had not been exposed to art just prior to this and had not had such a wonderful teacher who made me feel accomplished, my future would have been much different. There was much abuse in my home: verbal, physical, and for me, sexual. I realized at a young age that education was my way out.

When I was 12 I knew that I wanted to be an interior designer. I knew that I wanted to attend a design school in New York City—either Pratt Institute or Parsons School of Design. I started to write for brochures from the schools. Reading those brochures was my nightly regimen. I would reread about every course offered. It was my ticket out. I took as many art classes as I could fit in my schedule.

I wanted to take the first level art class during my freshman year of high school. This class was only offered first period. I had played the flute since fourth grade so the first period elective I had been signed up for was band. I made the decision to drop band if I could get into the art class. I had to personally go to the art teacher and beg her to let me into her class. She was not convinced that I was really interested in art. Many students would sign up for this class because they thought it was an easy grade. The class was full by the time I got there. I just remember promising her that she would not be sorry if she gave me the chance. I persisted and she finally let me into her class. I loved every minute of it.

Over the course of my high school life I enrolled in almost every art class that my high school offered. I joined the Art Club and I was voted "Most Artistic" by my senior class peers. My dream came true when I received a letter from Parsons School of Design (now named Parsons the New School for Design) stating that I had been accepted.

Studying at and graduating from Parsons was one of the hardest things that I ever had to do, but I loved it. My roommate and I became best friends and supported each other through the rigorous program. Three weeks after graduation, I went back upstate and married my high school sweetheart. I found a design job and started my dream career.

After 4 years of marriage we decided to start a family. We suffered through six years of infertility and heartache before we decided that adoption was the best route for us. Just before our 10th anniversary we were blessed with a beautiful baby girl.

It was at this time that my secrets began to wreak havoc on me. With the adoption of my daughter, the desire to break the chain of dysfunction became paramount. I had kept my secret for 20 years and it was time to get help. I enrolled in an Adult Children of Alcoholics (Dysfunctional Family) support group and also began individual therapy.

Over the next 7 years I was busy raising my daughter and working part-time. I loved doing art projects and crafts with my daughter. I would volunteer in her preschool and elementary school. I love being around children and I love to watch them be creative. When my daughter started elementary school, I had some time to finally take some art classes for myself. Even though I am an interior designer, which is a creative occupation in itself, I did not make the time to paint or create fine art. I was truly missing this in my life. I enjoyed painting for 2 years, and then we adopted our second child, a boy. Again, fine art was pushed into the background as other responsibilities became more important for me. My son was 3 when we moved to California.

During my first session at Art & Creativity for Healing, I was nervous but also excited. I had not painted in such a long time. What if my paintings were no good? So many thoughts rushed through my head. Laurie started the workshop and put everyone at ease. We painted the first warm up exercise. I did it! There was no stopping me now! When we got to the signature exercise titled "What's Going On?" I cried through the whole painting. I processed feelings that I had not had time to process or would not let myself process. When I left that day I knew that I had to come back. Laurie predicted that she would see more of me.

Like most people, we get busy with our day-to-day lives and forget to find time for ourselves. It took me a while to get back to Art & Creativity. I signed up for the Level One Instructor Training because I knew that I had to get more involved. I thoroughly enjoyed my training because it allowed time for me to be creative. When I came home with all of my pieces, both of my kids asked if they could go to a workshop at Art & Creativity for Healing. I volunteered at some of the workshops and I especially liked the sessions for children and young adults.

Volunteering opened up different opportunities for me. While attending the workshops I was busy processing my own feelings. Even though you are sitting next to people, you are so engrossed in your own process that you do not witness anyone else's. While volunteering you can see how others process. They may start with one color and by the end of the painting that area is completely painted over. I truly liked this aspect of volunteering.

Each time I attended a workshop or volunteered, it cemented my decision that I had to get more involved in Art & Creativity for Healing. I attended the Level Two Instructor Training, and when I went home I was asked, "When can we go to Art & Creativity?" I took out some paints, sponges, and Q-tips and as a family we started to create paintings. We were just experimenting with the paints and having fun. Shortly after my Level Two Training and one day before the Palette of Colors Fundraiser for Art & Creativity for Healing, I was diagnosed with Stage 2 breast cancer. I received a call from my doctor at 9:30 AM with the awful news: "You have breast cancer." At 11:00 AM I was in the surgeon's office, and at 1:30 PM I was in an MRI machine with magnets banging around my skull. Crazy thoughts were rushing through my head. I have three tumors that are pretty large. Is it in my nodes? How long do I have? Will I need a bilateral Mastectomy? What is chemotherapy like? Am I going to lose my hair? I started to cry.

When the first part of the MRI was completed, the technician came into the room and saw that I was crying. She was very compassionate but insisted for the next part of the exam I needed to be extremely still to get good results. She suggested that I think about something that did not make me cry.

I thought of being on the beach…and then I thought of my kids on the beach and started to cry. I thought of flowers…and then thought of my kids picking me flowers and I started to cry. I thought about Disneyland…and then started to think of my kids at Disneyland and began to cry. Nothing was working. I finally said, "I can do this." I started to think about painting a wash of color on a canvas.

I just kept painting different colors in long sweeping strokes. It worked. I made it through the exam. There were many exams and scans to follow. It worked every time.

While going through neoadjuvant chemotherapy, I brought my Art & Creativity journal with me. I could not bring paints but I brought colored pencils and markers. During a few of the treatments while the chemicals were coursing through my veins I would express what I was feeling in color. A red circle represented the chemotherapy-induced migraine. Yellow and brown for the tangle of plastic tubing that delivered the chemicals through my veins. Blue and green arrows were my hope to be cancer free someday. Brown lines represented my hair that had fallen out. Yellow was the warm, permeating sunshine that I love. Red represented the outpouring of love that I felt since my diagnosis. Pink—I have always loved pink, and now I wear the pink ribbon as a survivor of breast cancer.

Breast cancer as well as many other diseases affects the whole family, not just the patient. My case was no different. The diagnosis and treatment had been hard on all of us. This was a perfect time for my children to get their chance to go to Art & Creativity for Healing. We attended a Sunday afternoon "Expressing Feelings with Color" workshop facilitated by Laurie. We had a wonderful time and the workshop was beneficial to all of us. It gave me and my children a way to visually express the varied feelings that we had been dealing with for many months.

All of us were dealing with the same disease but feeling our own emotions. It gave my 13-year-old daughter a safe place to express what she was feeling. She had always written in a journal, but this was a different way for her to process her feelings and questions about this disease. My 6-year-old son also enjoyed the workshop. He was shy at first, but he had very definitive expressions of his emotions about breast cancer, and seeing his mom sick and losing her hair. It has always been an interesting part of the creative process for me to see many people using the same medium and subject matter and all creating such individual pieces of art. This was no different. We all processed our feelings about breast cancer but as our experiences and emotions were different, so were our paintings.

We came home with a car filled with art and placed them all on the mantel to enjoy. People visiting our home have commented on how busy we must have been creating all of these paintings. Both children asked when they could attend another workshop!

I have taken many of the workshops offered at Art & Creativity for Healing. I have repeated some of the same exercises but always have different results. While our lives and the issues that we deal with in our lives change, our need to process emotions stays the same. I will continue to weave what I have learned from Laurie's processes throughout my life. I can only hope that I can make a contribution to help others the way that Art & Creativity for Healing has helped me and those that I love heal.

Mary Beth
Newport Beach, California

ERICA'S STORY

As a child, I had to grow up pretty quickly due to my parents' rough divorce and other difficult family issues. As a teenager I was raped, and I chose to keep it a secret. As a young adult, I entered into a marriage that became emotionally abusive and ended in divorce. After the separation, I immediately left the comforts of my long term home city and moved over 1000 miles south for a new beginning. I had always done an excellent job of moving forward, surviving, and planning ahead. However, I had never been able to enjoy the current moment, process and forgive the past, or focus on my dreams, spirituality, and real life purpose.

When I first arrived in Southern California, I felt alone a lot of the time (even though I spent extensive hours in the office each week) and quickly realized that I needed to stop feeling sorry for myself, start helping others, and create a more balanced life. I researched volunteer opportunities for weeks, but for one reason or another, things didn't pan out. Then, one day I checked my mailbox and the volunteer opportunity had found me! It was a local newspaper with a call for volunteers for Art & Creativity for Healing (later, I found out Laurie advertised only once with this newsletter). I ran inside, pulled up the website on my computer, and immediately signed up for the volunteer orientation. It was a magnetic calling to be connected with the organization. What I didn't know in that moment was how much the art programs would help heal my broken heart and change my life.

I started volunteer work (welcoming students, squeezing paint, setting up classes, et cetera) in April of 2006. In each session, I saw a fresh, yet broad set of emotions—ranging from sadness, anger, rage, fear, and loneliness to joy and excitement—as the participants powerfully released their colors onto the canvas. The dynamics of each class seemed to produce a unique yet similar experience for the participants. It was similar in a way that each person walked away continually processing the emotions they just expressed, and unique in the way that each person processed different emotions.

After several months passed, Laurie encouraged me to start the path of facilitating classes, so I signed up for the Art for Healing Certificate with Chapman University. Going through the Chapman program allowed me to release my emotions as well. The quarter-long program created tremendous healing and growth for me.

During the first session of the program, I felt an immediate spark. That flicker kept expanding and stirring feelings up in me for the remaining sessions. Other than talking with a few close friends over the years, I had never taken time to focus on the negative events that occurred in my life. I worked very hard to suppress much of what I was feeling. After completing the program, I had to take a "timeout". I needed to breathe and absorb all that had changed in my mind, heart, and soul. I continued to work through a long-needed healing process and now feel I am in a much healthier place. I can finally enjoy precious moments as they occur! I found I can do more in less time at work, which allows me to spend my evenings and weekends focusing on the people and activities I love.

The Bible talks about times in life when God has to really scrub your wounds to help you heal. Apparently, I was due for an intense scrubbing. I was truly blessed to land on the doorstep of Art & Creativity for Healing. I now understand that my life events helped to build my character, spirituality, and strength. My support from and involvement with Art & Creativity for Healing helped spring-board me onto a new path in life at a time when I stood at a major crossroads. This new path is free from fear, is purpose-driven, and is focused on helping others in a variety of capacities, including using art as an expression of feelings. I truly look at life in a new light, and I am deeply grateful for my ties to this organization. It has been a beautiful gift—a gift I am now able to share with others for a lifetime!

Erica
Aliso Viejo, California

NANCY'S STORY

My first Art & Creativity for Healing workshop was "Expressing Feelings with Color" at Mission Hospital. I went with a friend who I worked with holding workshops for the disabled community. On the way there we agreed that if we were lucky, we might glean something we could use in our workshops. We left changed people. I thoroughly enjoyed the process, and my friend found herself speechless over her painting, which expressed grief she had repressed over the death of a very dear friend years before. I immediately investigated the instructor training program.

As an instructor for various Art & Creativity for Healing programs over the past five years, I have learned that we all need healing. Personally, while doing the exercises, I have found that memories come to the surface, situations are revisited, and connections are made. The method of painting is direct and immediate, capturing the emotion of the moment—not the intellect—which is key. Art & Creativity for Healing gives us an avenue to express the emotions for which we often don't have words.

I find this is especially poignant in the bereavement classes. I was a widow at age 37, totally overwhelmed with a 9 year old daughter and a 7 year old son who had special needs. It was literally all I could do just to maintain, and all those feelings were very hard to communicate to someone who had not been in that situation and experienced the same. Despite the many years since I experienced such loss, over and over I see the surviving spouse or family member grapple with many of the same feelings I experienced. Guiding them through the four weeks of exercises, I watch them rediscover memories of moments they were no longer conscious of while they associate color to their feelings and eventually surprise themselves by looking to the future. It is a wonderful process and I feel so fortunate to be able to help these people who are finding their way through one of life's biggest tragedies.

At one recent workshop, one widow was stumped on how to paint her remembrance piece. She couldn't decide how to start, and was

getting frustrated. I suggested she choose a color, for no particular reason, and just begin to paint. She chose red and was quite surprised at what came out. Her late husband had been a fireman, and she realized that red reminded her of his truck and of her feelings of pride in him and his work. Red continued to play a part in reminding her of a number of past experiences they shared, like gardening, even a favorite shirt of his, and the painting became a comfort to her.

Another widow painted a jutting mountain in the middle of an ocean with five large trees, many smaller trees, and a lovely sunset. She explained that she realized her husband had been a huge source of strength for many people and that he was a sort of a "rock" for them all. The five trees were their immediate family and the many smaller trees were all the people that relied on her husband in a variety of ways. It was quite a tribute and one she said she wouldn't have been able to articulate before the painting.

Teens also respond particularly well to Art & Creativity for Healing. Because the projects ask questions, they are able to share issues that they might have been uncomfortable bringing up on their own. It provides another form of expression that makes it easier to talk about the issue.

One young lady found such beautiful pieces of blue for her collage, but just wasn't happy with how they were laid out. When she expressed her disappointment, I remarked that she had plenty of time left to rearrange them, which she did. She created a knockout beautiful piece that had a kind of cyclone feel to it and seemed very happy with it. It was all I could do not to stop her when she took a piece of tissue and glued it down, covering it all up. She later shared that this was how she felt, like there was a lot going on with her that no one ever saw because she felt she had to put up a front with people, essentially covering up all her feelings and her beauty. I was blown away.

A young man who hardly said a word during the class created this orange mark that rose and fell with a really long tail for a feeling he had that day. After coaxing him to share, he explained that he had a very long day ahead of him. I asked about the color and he simply stated he hated orange. It was a simple yet perfect visual description of what he was feeling.

Getting people to start thinking in color creates a new perspective. One woman from an Art & Creativity for Healing workshop said she had not worked in her visual journal that week because so much had happened, but she had thought in color every day! Her son had gotten in trouble and she just saw red! She was laughing but said it helped her identify how she felt, and she even got over it faster.

A young woman who had left her husband and son in Mexico to help take care of her sister undergoing cancer treatments painted a single blue flower when the project asked her to paint an imaginary garden. She was surprised to realize how lonely she felt and how much she missed her family. Her sister was in the workshop as well and it was a gentle eye-opener for them both.

I also work with the "Visiting Art Angel Bedside Program" at Children's Hospital Orange County (CHOC) in Orange, California. We work with the children on the Oncology/Hematology floor, especially those who are in isolation or Intensive Care. This program is a "one on one" art program that gives the children an opportunity to do some "normal" kid-type activities. We created an art gallery where we hang framed paintings for everyone on the floor to enjoy. One painting displays the work of two sisters, each painting their interpretation of the pain of sickle cell disease. They are very different. Even the little ones understand the power of expressing feelings with color and shapes, which often enables them to describe things they didn't think they could talk about.

Since many of the kids we see at CHOC are experiencing the difficult trauma of their disease, we also do fun craft activities. Learning a new skill or having success with a new material is often reason enough for them to sit up and play awhile with us. Art & Creativity for Healing offers participants an opportunity to experiment with different media and to try it out in a relevant project—not a technique-orientated project, but a process-oriented one. How will you know if this material speaks to you if you don't get a chance to really use it and explore its properties in a non-threatening setting? Along the way, sometimes your perspective shifts. While painting a stress management project, one gentleman realized that what he had seen as problems were really just situations that would change in time. One therapist surprised herself by coming to the realization that the thing she would give up first in her life was something she hadn't even considered a source of stress!

It is unusual to find a program that speaks to each person differently. The genius of the projects is that they ask leading, but open-ended questions so each participant can relate it to their very specific experiences or feelings. The projects open a door, and each person gets to decide which door it is for them, and how far they want to go inside. Each and every class is truly an adventure.

Nancy
Mission Viejo, California

ELIZABETH'S STORY

After losing my twin boys shortly after their birth in 2001, I participated in individual therapy sessions, attended countless grief workshops, and read as many books as I could get my hands on, yet I was still angry—at myself, but mostly at God.

By God's grace I was led to Art & Creativity for Healing. In 2002, we sat next to Laurie Zagon and her husband, Joe Sorrentino, during a performance of the Broadway Series at the Orange County Performing Arts Center. We hit it off right away, and Laurie invited us to attend an Art for Healing workshop.

At the end of the workshop, we were asked to express our feelings by using acrylic paint to create a "Window to My Heart". During that exercise, I cried more deeply than I had in years.

After that initial workshop, I signed up for two more, but it was two years before I could return. During that time, Laurie generously forwarded my credit and continued to gently remind me that the door was open when I was ready to come back.

Unfortunately, my grief led to illness and after seeing many doctors and specialists with varied diagnoses, I realized that I needed to stop blaming myself and God for what had happened. I finally made my way back to Art & Creativity for Healing and took one of Laurie's "Art for Healing Bereavement" workshops for adults.

One of the first things I noticed was the tenderness and understanding of the other participants in the workshop. Even to this day, I can still recall the losses recounted by the other participants. I was moved by empathy and cried for their losses, but when it came time to share, I was speechless. I cried silently, and struggled to find words as Laurie continued to comfort and reassure me. It was then that I realized the impact of the pain I felt because my mother did not come to the hospital with me or visit after the boys died. She lived in Chicago, but my father and stepmother, who live in Virginia, still made it out to visit in November of that year.

I also began to realize that my desire to control everything had taken an even greater toll on my emotional health and wellbeing.

My experiences in the "Art for Healing Bereavement" workshop, and the release I experienced through the use of color and shapes went well beyond what any book, seminar, or grief workshop had ever accomplished. I am still amazed how this class was able to access a core that no therapist, friend, or family member had ever touched.

Art & Creativity for Healing was able to help me identify the emotional triggers that were causing my grief and sadness, and as a result, a whole new "me" emerged. It is very important to me to share my story so that others can benefit from Art & Creativity for Healing's methods. After participating in their workshops, I now believe that emotions are unconsciously linked to colors and shapes, and can often only be unlocked by using paint on canvas.

Professionally, I am an attorney, but I have found another outlet for my emotions—mosaic crosses. I started working with mosaics in April of 2006, and have already participated in two art shows—the Camarillo Fall Art Festival in September of 2006, and the 3rd Annual Art Exhibit for the California State Bar Association Annual Meeting, which was held in October of 2006 in Monterey, California.

It is only through the grace of God which connected me with Art & Creativity for Healing that I continue on my path back toward God's abundant love and mercy.

Elizabeth
Costa Mesa, California

RANDI'S STORY

I came to Art & Creativity for Healing first as a student in the Beginning Creativity series. It was at a particularly difficult time in my life. My mother had recently passed away after a long and difficult illness, and I had also just gone through a painful divorce.

In my work as an elementary school teacher I was feeling tired and burnt out. As an artist I felt stuck and unproductive—I would just go into my studio and stare at my paints. It was a time in my life when I knew I needed to change directions but I still did not know which way to go. The Beginning Creativity class was truly a new beginning for me. During the four-week class, I began to feel back in touch with the playful, creative side of myself—this energy was soon revitalizing all other aspects of my life.

I began taking every class that Art & Creativity for Healing offered. I loved it so much that I wanted to become an instructor. I found it exciting to help people get in touch with their own images and to learn how to use Art for Healing. I am currently working on my master's degree in counseling psychology, and I believe more than ever in the power of the image to facilitate healing and personal growth.

I have enjoyed teaching all kinds of classes for Art & Creativity for Healing. Not every group is open and receptive at first, but over time I have seen their resistance fade as they engage with the art and experience the power of this work. The following is an account of a class I taught at Hoag Hospital. It shows how even the most resistant group can benefit from the use of Art & Creativity and Healing's methods.

It was a class for teens. Tony arrived first, signed in, and sat down with Eddie and Rita. There were a few missing students but it was time to start. Just as I was about to close the door Tiffany arrived, talking on her cell phone and sipping a coffee drink. I told her she would need to turn off her cell phone once we began. She rolled her eyes at me and said, "Whatever", snapping her cell phone shut.

As I looked around the room I was met with stares that ranged from hostility to boredom. During the introductions they all made it clear they were only there because their parents made them come, and they all wanted me to know they hated art—except for Tony, he liked graffiti and tagging. I took a deep breath and thought, "Tough crowd". Then I remembered other groups of teens I had worked with at Art & Creativity for Healing. I knew better than to expect cheerful cooperation, especially for the first meeting—enthusiasm is just not cool.

I explained that our project was going to be a collage about our fears. I had brought magazines and colored tissue paper for them to use. We talked a little bit about our fears and what they might be. Not surprisingly Tony looked at me and said, "I ain't afraid of nuthin'." Eddie said, "Oh man, I wanna go home." Rita started crying and Tiffany continued to look at the ceiling and said, "OK, let's just get this over with." There were heavy sighs as they began taking magazines. As they got involved in the work I noticed the atmosphere in the room slowly began to shift. As they finished their collages, I was astounded at what I saw.

Tony volunteered to go first. He had cut out a lot of black and white arrows and had made them go in circles on his paper. Then he had cut out blobs of red tissue paper and glued them around the arrows. I asked him to tell me about his collage. He was hesitant at first, but he finally said it was about his life, and how he is in a cycle he can't get out of: doing drugs, beating people up, and doing jail time. He said he was stuck; he could not stop doing those things. "The red blobs are for blood, 'cause I'll probably get killed on the street sometime," he said matter-of-factly.

Next was Eddie. I noticed his collage had a big pig on it, the kind that said, "Oink". He told me the pig was about a policeman. He said he was afraid of cops, because one called him the N-word. I did not know the particulars of the incident, but to Eddie the fear was real and he wanted to put it on his paper. It was the first time he had spoken all afternoon. Rita shook her head at me; she did not want to share. I asked her how making the collage was for her, and she replied, "Hard, it was hard." I told her if she changed her mind she could talk about it later.

Laurie Zagon

I looked at her images and there were lots of kids and tear drops glued around the page and a heart with a line through it. I could only imagine what her sadness was, but I knew that for her it was very real. She was not ready to talk about it, but she did want the group to see it, the first step towards sharing her feelings.

Last was Tiffany. Her collage had some pictures of beautiful women with lots of turquoise tissue surrounding them. I was puzzled what might be fearful there and I asked her to tell me about it. She said that she was afraid of not being thin and beautiful. She said getting fat was her biggest fear, worse than anything. I asked her why the turquoise and she said, "It's a boring color. I eat when I'm bored and I'm bored A LOT!" For not wanting to do the collage, these kids had done some amazing work.

I have found that the power of Art & Creativity for Healing is that it allows people to get in touch with their feelings and express what is going on in their lives. Whether people are dealing with illness, fear, abuse, or just daily stress, using art in this way allows them to use tools such as color, shape, texture, and line to come to terms with issues in their lives. What comes out is not necessarily pretty or "good" in the way we are usually taught to think of art, but it is a process that allows those who utilize it to express emotions they may not have known existed. It is powerful work and a privilege to be a witness of this healing process for people.

As Tony, Eddie, Rita, and Tiffany left the session that day I felt that some important things had happened. They had not wanted to do the fear collage and yet they did it. In talking about their collages, they had shared some insights about their lives. They may not have been pretty or sweet, but they were real. It was a place for us to begin.

Randi
Laguna Niguel, California

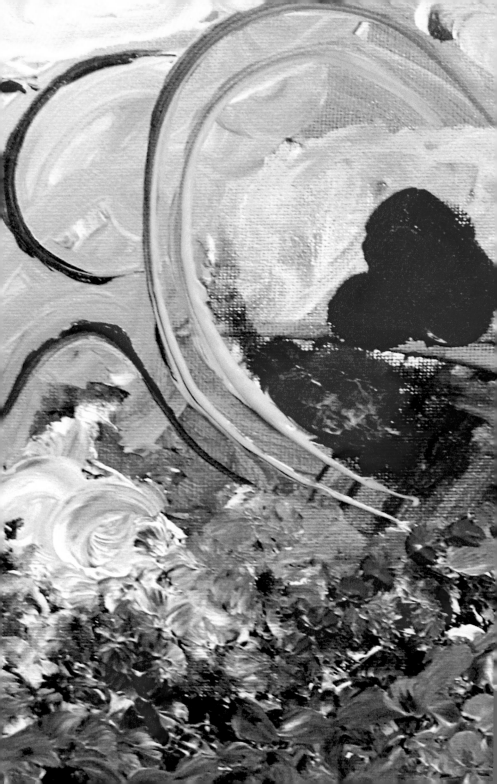

JESSICA'S STORY

The last week of February 2014, I was sent to Camp Pendleton to be attached to MAG-39 (Marine Aircraft Group). My mission was to attend the In/Out Patient program for further recovery. Resistant at first, I just wanted to make it through the eight weeks in the hopes that I would be able to continue on with my career. Attending the counseling sessions and group classes helped, but after having been through two rehabilitations, obviously something was missing that was not allowing me to continue to heal.

When I arrived and began the In/Out Patient program, I was pleased to find out that there were art, dance, yoga, and tai chi classes available each day. Dancing was something I already knew helped me stay balanced since it was my career prior to the Marine Corps. Yoga and tai chi, which involved the use of connecting the mind and body, was also something I was familiar with and found comfort in. Then I discovered the Art for Healing class. I remembered loving art in elementary school, but I hadn't done anything remotely close to art since I was that young.

When I arrived to my first Art for Healing workshop, I found the tables set up in a horseshoe shape. They were covered in plastic and individual place settings for twelve people were already set up. At each place there was a plastic apron, a bottle of water, a cup, a plate, sponges, Q-tips, a paper towel, and many small containers—each with a different color acrylic paint inside.

Throughout the class we were instructed to paint with different prompts. We did not have an object to look at to paint—we were to paint our feelings. Sometimes we could use only one or two colors to illustrate the emotions that were brought up inside of us as we listened to each prompt. This is much harder than it sounds. Personally, I found great joy in painting things that were happy or that made me feel good. When asked to paint about fear, pain, sadness, anger—this is where it became difficult for me. Coming in to this eight week In/Out Patient program, I did not want to dig deep into my feelings. I was tired of reliving the past two years over and over again.

When I was asked to paint these difficult feelings, I found that it was doing me no good keeping them shoved deep down inside. As I would paint these emotions, the memories would surface, the tears would begin to fill my eyes, and I could feel some of the same sensations I had felt when I had gone through those trying times. This allowed me to open up more in the group discussion and let out some of what I was bottling up.

After a couple weeks, I began to realize how great I felt after the Art for Healing classes and decided to stop by Michael's to pick up some canvas and paint to bring to my room. Practically every day and every weekend I would spend time painting. Although I was not painting feelings, I found that finding images online that would be fun to create or creating my own works brought just as much satisfaction and emotional release. The time spent in front of the canvas gave me time to meditate and lower my anxiety level. I loved being able to go to my room at lunch after a rough morning of sessions or being able to do the same at the end of the day and release it all through being creative.

By the time my eight weeks were drawing to a close at Camp Pendleton, the majority of my room's wall space was covered with my paintings from the Art for Healing classes and with art I had created on my free time. When it was time to go back to Yuma, I was not looking forward to returning. Being at Camp Pendleton, removed from reminders such as people, places, and things had helped, but the thought of being plopped right in the middle of all of it again made me sick to my stomach. Dread would wash through me with the thought of it. Before arriving in Yuma I had put on a positive mindset and was determined that I could stand taller and stronger there.

The day I arrived back in Yuma, my Command had no idea I was coming back. There was no place for me and they weren't sure where I supposed to go. I was accused of not contacting the unit while I was away and sat in the Administration office for almost two hours. Needless to say, by that point the positive mindset walked out the door and it felt as though I had never left. All the feelings of hatred, disappointment, sadness, and anxiety crept back in. I hadn't even been back for half a day and I was already ready to flip a table in anger.

Other disappointments and frustrations have surfaced since my return to Yuma, but it is different now because I have an outlet to express myself through painting. I always make sure that I have paint and canvas on hand. For the first several weeks back in Yuma, I would paint during my lunch break and after work as well. Besides the gym, it has been the only thing to calm me, level me, and help me find a balanced, positive spot in my life.

As a couple of months have passed, people began to see my artwork during room inspections or when I would randomly post one on Facebook. I created a few Disney characters for my friend's children and a couple of other paintings upon request. Several times the question was brought up whether I was starting to make commission on them and that I should because they were very good. Never in my wildest dreams did I think that I would be able to sell art pieces of my own creation.

One day I was asked to paint Winnie the Pooh characters for a baby room and be paid for my work. I agreed and then really started to wonder if I could do this. I had originally started a blog and thought this would also be a great place to display my artwork. I posted paintings and then advertised my blog on Facebook. Within 10 minutes someone wanted to buy two pieces! I sold more and more and eventually started to receive requests for specific works. So far I have sold twelve pieces and hope that I am able to continue. With the recent paintings sold I have decided to start giving 10% of the profit to the Edith Sanford Breast Cancer Foundation. It only feels right to give something to a good cause with being blessed enough to be able to sell things I've created.

If it weren't for the Art for Healing class in Camp Pendleton, I'm not sure I'd be in the mental and physical shape I am in now. Thank you so much for such a wonderful and rewarding opportunity. I am forever grateful for this healing tool.

Jessica
Oceanside, California

JENNIFER'S STORY

The first time I spoke with Laurie I knew I had found something special. I had been looking for a way to combine my art background, my passion for people in recovery, and a desire to serve a particular group of young men in a residential treatment center in Arkansas. Up until that moment I had no knowledge of Art for Healing…and no real appreciation for abstract painting either.

I had studied graphic design in college, worked briefly as a graphic artist until I had my three sons, and had been working as a professional artist with oil paintings at Mission Fine Art Gallery. Through my son's struggle with drugs and alcohol about 4 years ago, I was introduced to a whole world of amazing, courageous people who were fighting for their lives in recovery. I became absorbed with learning all I could about addiction in its many forms and the paths to recovery.

The Art for Healing Certificate Program was exactly what I needed. I was looking for a way for my work to serve a greater purpose, and to use what I have personally experienced as an artist and teacher about the transformational power of art. With this program I did not have to be a therapist—I could be myself—an artist with a heart for people who are willing to do whatever it takes to get well. In the intensive training, we were taught that it was not about us, but rather it was about facilitating a healing process. I believed that if my heart was right, this would be my ministry, not a job. With Art & Creativity for Healing I felt like I was generously given all the information, training, support, and opportunities that I needed to start my ministry.

I founded HEart HEALS and held my first workshop in October 2011. Mariners Church gave me their blessing as a Care & Recovery ministry and I began running monthly workshops on their campus. I was witnessing firsthand how creativity, spirituality, and loving people intersected to support recovery! I have provided annual workshops for an after-school mentoring program in Watts and for a men's sober living home in Huntington Beach. In April, I was hired to run weekly art groups for a women's outpatient treatment center. I am actually doing what I set out to do.

As an artist, I've always been drawn to painting the stories of people I see around me. Now I'm honored to be able to help people abstractly paint their own stories. They paint stories of grief and loss, struggle and ambivalence, but also stories of how relationships, love, and hope fit into the beautiful picture of their lives. Every time I am a witness to someone's story, I feel that I am the one who is blessed.

Jennifer
Newport Beach, California

CLAUDIA'S STORY

Whenever I facilitate a workshop, I am witness to little blessings which confirm the power of Art for Healing. Workshop participants are always so appreciative that we show up with art supplies in hand and smiles on our faces. They appreciate that we take time out of our lives to help them learn a little something about themselves through art. What they don't know is that we, as facilitators, are also learning a little something about ourselves along the way.

Everything changes the moment I start facilitating a workshop. When the participants walk into the classroom, my purpose becomes clear. I am there to encourage them to express themselves courageously. Somehow, all problems or exhaustion from the week disappear. It is one of the best parts of doing something you love. Time seems to stand still. I feel blessed to be the person to guide them through the workshop, and they in turn feel special to be a part of it.

Our classroom becomes a safe place in which the participants are able to simply be and express through painting what they are carrying with them that day. The workshop gives them a couple hours during the day to truly connect with themselves, see their circumstances from a distance, and express their emotions on canvas without judgment. It sounds simple in writing, but in fact there are many little things that we do as facilitators that give them permission to experiment creatively, quiet their mind, and accept their painted mark....especially in the midst of tears.

The workshop I facilitate is called "Paint to Feel, Paint to Heal". Like all Art for Healing facilitators, I guide the participants to express their feelings with paint on canvas, but in the act of doing this; we guide them to do a whole lot more. We guide them to quiet their minds, find their center, and come into the present moment. We guide them to be aware of the thoughts which may sabotage the process. We guide them to take deep calming breaths. We guide them to visualize their emotions, which are individual to their experience, and to give them form with painted dabs of color.

Guiding someone to use paint as a modality of self-expression is an immediately rewarding experience. I get to witness how every participant builds up their courage the moment they choose their color and make their mark on the canvas.

I am touched that, in the midst of so much uncertainty in their lives, these participants are willing to try something new, with a complete stranger to guide them through it.

There is something incredibly beautiful in the participants' sharing about their finished paintings. There are moments in which the they paint with tremendous heart. Their pain is present in the way they choose to make their painted mark, sometimes expressed through thick, jagged strokes which may symbolize the intensity of their emotion. At other times, their marks may be veil-like and shy.

We take nothing for granted in these classes. Most of these participants have struggled with damaged relationships from the time they were children. It is foreign to them to have someone respect them, honor them by giving them time and space, and validate them with simple affirmations such as a smile and a warm look as they courageously and vulnerably tell their story without words by painting abstractly on canvas.

I am blessed and strengthened by their courage to continue on and change the path of their lives. Thank you to all who have allowed me to show them the healing power of expression that lives inside all of us.

Claudia
Costa Mesa, California

PART FIVE
Community Collaboration

One of the things I recognized early on was how little money there was within the nonprofit agency budget to pay for art programs. Whenever I would ask hospitals and agencies if they had a budget for workshops, the answer was usually no.

Because I wanted to reach as many children and families as possible with my Art for Healing programs, funded or not, I began collecting as many art supplies as I possibly could to use for my initial workshops. I spent a lot of time trying to find ways to pay for supplies — my husband and I financed a lot of the cost of these supplies in the early years just to get things started.

I did have a wonderful connection in 1990 with an acrylic paint company out of New York that donated quite a bit of paint, which got us through many of our children's workshops. As I facilitated workshops, my friends asked to volunteer or to donate money for art supplies. A twenty dollar donation paid for the art supplies for 34 children, in those early days.

The passion that I felt about the Art for Healing work, along with my faith helped me to believe that the funds I needed would ultimately be there. In fact, the funds always came in even at the most desperate times. I remember one day teaching a class and mentioning in the class that things were difficult financially and that I wanted to work with abused children, but was waiting for the necessary funds to come in. That day there was a wealthy woman in the class who went home and mailed me a check for $5,000. Her note said, "Keep up the good work!"

The agencies listed below represent important partnerships that I have formed over the last 10 years. Most of these programs have been funded by individuals like the woman mentioned above, as well as from corporation and foundation grants. I recommend to anyone wanting to engage others in their work to spend a lot of time speaking to everyone they know about their passion. You never know who might be listening.

The following are agencies we have partnered with to-date:

AIDS Services Foundation Orange County—Irvine
Men, women, children, and families in Orange County living with HIV /AIDS

AIDS Service Foundation—Irvine
Men, women, and children living with HIV/AIDS

Armed Services YMCA—San Diego
Wounded warriors and their families

Big Brothers/Big Sisters of Orange County
At-risk youth

Boys & Girls Clubs of Garden Grove—Laguna Beach & Tustin
At-risk youth and their families

Casa Teresa—Orange
Single, pregnant women

Camp Pendleton Marine Base
Children and their families affected by military deployments

Canyon Acres—Anaheim Hills
Abused children

Children's Hospital Orange County (CHOC)
Children suffering from leukemia and other life threatening
illnesses and their families

CSP Community Service Programs—Santa Ana
Sexual assault victim services and domestic violence assistance programs

Families and Communities Together (F.a.C.T)—Orange

Family Resource Centers for underprivileged children and families

Anaheim-Fullerton FRC—Anaheim

Corbin Family Resource Center—Santa Ana

Friendly Center FRC—Orange

La Habra FRC—La Habra

Magnolia Park FRC—Garden Grove

Minnie St FRC—Santa Ana

Oak View FRC—Huntington Beach Ponderosa Park FRC—Anaheim Anaheim Harbor FRC—Anaheim

South Orange County FRC—Lake Forest

Stanton FRC—Stanton

Tustin FRC—Tustin

Westminster FRC—Westminster

Girls Inc.—Costa Mesa

At-risk girls

Human Options Shelter—Irvine

Abused women, counselors and staff

Mariposa Women's Center—Orange

Bereavement workshops for children and adults

Mercy House/Emmanuel House—Santa Ana

Homeless with HIV/AIDS

Mission Hospital—Mission Viejo and Laguna Niguel

Families coping with illness or grief and staff retreats

Olive Crest—Santa Ana

Abused children

Orange County Department of Education
Economically disadvantaged youth and juvenile offenders participating in the Alternative, Community, and Correctional Education Schools, and Services (ACCESS) Program
Academic Center of Tustin
Greeley School—Orange
Joplin School—Trabuco Canyon
Project Hope School—Orange
Santiago Creek School—Santa Ana
Shaefer School—Orange

Orangewood Children's Foundation—Orange
Foster youth

Pathway School—Lake Forest
Children with developmental challenges

Pepperdine University—Culver City and Irvine
Doctoral and masters candidates in psychology

Phoenix House—Santa Ana
Teens in recovery from substance abuse

Project ACCESS—Torrance
Underprivileged senior citizens

Project Hope Alliance—Costa Mesa
Homeless children

Shanti OC—Laguna Hills
Men, women, children, and families in Orange County living with HIV/AIDS

St. Joseph Health System—Orange
Cancer patients and their families

The Wooden Floor—Santa Ana
At-risk youth and their families

PART SIX
Partner Agency Statistics

Below are the 2014 Executive Reports from some of our partner agencies: Camp Pendleton, Human Options, and our Homelessness Programs.

CAMP PENDLETON - January 2011 to June 2014

Introduction
Doctors Nonprofit Consulting (DNC) was hired by Art & Creativity for Healing, Inc. (ACFH) in June of 2014 to provide an outcome evaluation for the program's Camp Pendleton Marine Corps Base (CPMCB) ACFH workshops held between January 2011 and June 2014. ACFH facilitates these "Art for Healing" workshop programs at more than 40 hospitals, treatment centers, military bases, and non-profit agencies throughout Southern California. Since 2000, more than 45,000 children and adults have participated in these classes and workshops.

Method
For this project, ACFH staff entered the data from their surveys into an online computer program. DNC then downloaded data spreadsheets in both excel and SPSS formats. DNC reviewed the data and addressed any data entry concerns with ACFH staff. SPSS statistical software was used for the evaluation process which was conducted by consultants in June and July of 2014. For this project, the program's data collection procedures were reviewed.

Data Set
The 2011-2014 data set consists of 1355 responses by 1086 adults and 269 children referred by CPMCB who received ACFH services between the period of January 2011 and June 2014. Generally when working with statistical evaluation, we like to see a large sample. Data sets of this size (n=1355) are generally regarded to be an accurate indicator of the measured items.

Statistics

Caucasians make up 57% of program participants and Hispanic/Latino Americans make up another 17%. Oceanside was the city of residence that most of the adult and child workshop participants resided in with San Clemente (11%) being the next highest.

Ninety-three percent of the adult workshops were titled: "Camp Pendleton Wounded Warriors." All workshops provided to children were "Expressing Feelings with Color". The top two psychological reasons reported by adult participants for taking a workshop were anxiety/stress (76%) and depression/sadness (66%). The top two reasons for children participants were that they liked art (46%) and divorce (31%). Almost a third of the children also indicated that someone they loved died (23%), sadness (23%), and anxiety/stress (23%) as reasons for taking a workshop.

Seventy-nine percent of adult participants and 78% of children strongly agreed that the workshop helped them express their emotions or share their feelings, and 78% of adults and 84% of children strongly agreed that they felt better after the workshop.

Eighty-four percent of adults and 77% of children of the participants strongly agreed that they would refer a friend or family member to this workshop. Furthermore, 84% of adults and 91% of children strongly agreed that they themselves would take another workshop from the program. Overall, it is significant to say that 99% of adults and 97% of children of the CPMCB participants that completed the survey were satisfied with their workshop.

Key Findings

The top two psychological reasons that CPMCB adult participants took the 2011-2014 workshops were anxiety or stress (76%) and depression/sadness (66%).

Seventy-nine percent of the CPMCB base adult participants strongly agreed that the workshop was great, 79% strongly agreed that the workshop helped them express their emotions, and 78% strongly agreed that they felt better after the workshop.

Ninety percent of the San Onofre Elementary School base child participants strongly agreed that the workshop was great, 78% strongly agreed that the workshop helped them share their feelings, and 84% strongly agreed that they felt better after the workshop.

Ninety-nine percent of adults and 97% of children of the CPMCB participants that completed the survey were satisfied with their workshop. Adult participants are more likely to refer a friend/family member (97%) than children (90%). Furthermore, 91% of children and 84% of adults strongly agreed that they themselves would take another workshop from the program.

HUMAN OPTIONS - June 2011 to June 2014

Introduction
Doctors Nonprofit Consulting (DNC) was hired by Art & Creativity for Healing, Inc. (ACFH) in June of 2014 to provide an outcome evaluation for the program's 2011-2014 Human Options participant data in ACFH workshops. ACFH facilitates these "Art for Healing" workshop programs at more than 40 hospitals, treatment centers, military bases, and non-profit agencies throughout Southern California. Since 2000, more than 45,000 children and adults have participated in these classes and workshops.

Method
For this project, ACFH staff entered the data from their surveys into an online computer program. DNC then downloaded data spreadsheets in both excel and SPSS formats. DNC reviewed the data and addressed any data entry concerns with ACFH staff. SPSS statistical software was used for the evaluation process which was conducted by consultants in June and July of 2014. For this project, the program's data collection procedures were reviewed.

Data Set
This data set consists of responses by 765 Human Options referred individuals who received ACFH services between the period of June 2011 and June 2014.

Generally when working with statistical evaluation, we like to see a large sample. Data sets of this size (n=765) are generally regarded to be an accurate indicator of the measured items.

Statistics
Hispanic/Latino(a) Americans made up 46% and Caucasians made up 35% of program participants. Irvine was the city of residence for most (88%) of the workshop participants due to the location of the shelter.

"Expressing Feelings with Color" was the title of 76% of workshops while "Paint to Feel, Paint to Heal" was the title of another 22%. The top two psychological reasons reported by participants for taking a workshop was abuse (87%) followed by depression/sadness (29%).

Eighty-four percent strongly agreed that the workshop was better than expected, 79.4% strongly agreed that the workshop helped them express their emotions, and 77.7% strongly agreed that they felt better after the workshop. Eighty-five percent of workshop participants also strongly agreed that the instructor was approachable and seemed to care about them. Eighty-five percent of participants strongly agreed that the instructor was on time.

Ninety-six percent of the Human Option participants that completed the survey were satisfied with their workshop. Eighty-two percent of the participants strongly agreed that they would refer a friend or family member to this workshop. Furthermore, 80% strongly agreed that they themselves would take another workshop from the program.

Key Findings
Eighty-four percent of Human Options participants strongly agreed that the workshop was better than expected, 79.4% strongly agreed that the workshop helped them express their emotions, and 78% strongly agreed that they felt better after the workshop.

Ninety-six percent of the participants that completed the survey were satisfied with their workshop. Eighty-two percent of participants strongly agreed that they would refer a friend or family member to this workshop. Furthermore, 79.5% strongly agreed that they themselves would take another workshop from the program.

The top two psychological reasons reported by Human Options participants for taking a workshop between 2011 and 2014 were abuse (87%) followed by anxiety/stress (33.5%) and depression (29.3%).

The evaluations indicated an overall agreement that the Art & Creativity for Healing instructors are caring and that participants are satisfied overall with the workshops.

HOMELESSNESS PROGRAMS - June 2011 to August 2014

Introduction
Doctors Nonprofit Consulting (DNC) was hired by Art & Creativity for Healing, Inc. (ACFH) in June of 2014 to provide an outcome evaluation for the program's 2011-2014 Homeless Program (HP) data for participants in ACFH workshops. ACFH facilitates these "Art for Healing" workshop programs at more than 40 hospitals, treatment centers, military bases, and non-profit agencies throughout Southern California. Since 2000, more than 45,000 children and adults have participated in these classes and workshops.

Method
For this project, ACFH staff entered the data from their surveys into an online computer program. DNC then downloaded data spreadsheets in both excel and SPSS formats. DNC reviewed the data and addressed any data entry concerns with ACFH staff. SPSS statistical software was used for the evaluation process which was conducted by consultants in August and September of 2014. For this project, the program's data collection procedures were reviewed. Initially, a series of frequency tables were run to establish basic program statistics. Following this, a series of correlations and one-way analysis of variance (ANOVA) tests were computed on the data. A full statistical report of the test outcomes is included in appendix A. Correlations are useful in determining how closely one variable relates to another variable. ANOVAs are useful for comparing differences between groups.

Data Set
This data set consists of responses by 336 HP referred individuals who received ACFH services between the period of June 2011 and June 2014. Generally when working with statistical evaluation, we like

to see a large sample. Data sets of this size (n=336) are generally regarded to be an accurate indicator of the measured items.

Statistics

Thirty-five percent of participants were adult and the remaining 65% were children/teens. Ages ranged from 8-33, with the average age of adult participants being 31.47 while the average age of child participants was 8.4 years of age.

Caucasians made up 47% of adult participants followed by Hispanic/Latino(a) American at 33%. Fifty-four percent of the child program participants did not list their ethnicity. Of those that did, Hispanic/Latino(a) American made up 82% of child participants followed by Caucasians at 10%.

Tustin was the city of residence for 68% of the adult workshop participants followed by Santa Ana at 17%. Seventy-nine percent of the child program participants did not list their city of residence. Of those that did, Stanton was 96%. These locations were used by participants due to the location of the shelter they were living in at the time.

"Expressing Feelings with Color" was the title of 86% of workshops. The top reason that adult participants took workshops was homelessness (58%) followed by own interest (28%).The majority of the child program participants did not list a reason for attending. Of those that did, it was because of homelessness (91%) followed by someone I love died (5%).

Eighty-five percent of adult and 77% of child participants strongly agreed that the workshop helped them express their emotions. Eighty-six percent of adult and 84% of child participants strongly agreed that they felt better after the workshop. Ninety-two percent of adults strongly agreed that the instructor was approachable. Additionally, 89% of child participants thought the instructor seemed to care about them.

Ninety-nine percent of the adult and 96% of child HP participants were satisfied with their workshop. For future workshops, 92% of the adult and 77% of child participants strongly agreed that they would refer a friend or family member to this workshop. Furthermore, 89% of adult and 89% of child participants strongly agreed that they themselves would take another workshop from the program.

Key Findings

Ninety-nine percent of the adult and 96% of child HP participants were satisfied with their workshop.

Eighty-five percent of adult and 77% of child HP participants strongly agreed that the workshop helped them express their emotions. Eighty-six percent of adult and 84% of child participants strongly agreed that they felt better after the workshop.

Ninety-two percent of the adult and 77% of child participants strongly agreed that they would refer a friend or family member to this workshop. Furthermore, 89% of all participants strongly agreed that they themselves would take another workshop from the program.

The top psychological reason that adult HP participants took workshops was homelessness (58%) followed by own interest (28%). The majority of the child program participants did not list a reason for attending. Of those that did, it was because of homelessness (91%) followed by someone I love died (5%).

The evaluations indicated an overall agreement that the ACFH instructors are approachable and caring.

EPILOGUE

Art & Creativity for Healing Inc. was formally incorporated in November of 2000 after operating as a volunteer effort, with no paid staff, for more than 10 years. Our mission is to facilitate Art for Healing workshops for children and adults suffering from abuse, illness, grief, or stress onsite, at hospitals, and at nonprofit facilities. Our programs address the emotional and social aspects of these conditions via the language of color and painting and provide encouragement and motivation for individuals living with them.

Art & Creativity for Healing workshops have helped thousands of individuals—those with chronic and life-threatening illnesses, at-risk and underprivileged youth, and those recovering from child abuse, substance abuse, and gang-related trauma—deal more effectively with the emotional, spiritual, and physical distresses caused by events in their lives. By expressing themselves creatively, participants can document their experience in a profound way, thus creating a healing environment for themselves. Byproducts of the art experience are greater self-awareness, the confidence to process feelings and emotions, and the ability to articulate and share these feelings and emotions with others.

Other therapeutic programs using art employ a loose format of free expression. Art & Creativity for Healing provides a structured approach of guided art exercises designed to elicit a creative response that encourages the release of stress issues, grief, anger, and shame.

Art & Creativity for Healing Inc. is governed by a Board of Directors comprised of individuals who have demonstrated capacity for leadership by attending the organization's classes and workshops, promoting the organization and its services and activities, fundraising, and acting as an advocate for the organization.

Since its incorporation in November of 2000, Art & Creativity for Healing Inc. has served over 50,000 individuals and partnered with more than 35 Orange County nonprofit agencies.

Laurie Zagon

Additionally, 500 artists, counselors, teachers, therapists, and medical professionals have been trained as facilitators through the organization's training program.

At Art & Creativity for Healing we believe:

• The act of painting can function as a separate language and contribute to the emotional healing process.

• The particular language of art creates the ability to communicate.

• The utilization of the creative process through painting can be healing and therapeutic.

• The artistic expression of emotions is good for our communities and our culture.

RESOURCES

The following is a list of some of my favorite books that have provided inspiration and guidance for me, and my work, over the years.

1. Black, Claudia. It's Never Too Late To Have a Happy Childhood: Inspirations for Inner Healing. Ballantine, 1989.

2. Cameron, Julia. The Artists Way. Tarcher, 1992.

3. Drucker, Peter F. Managing the Nonprofit Organization. Collins, 2006

4. Edwards, Betty. The New Drawing on the Right Site of the Brain. Putnam, 1999.

5. Fritz, Robert. The Path of Least Resistance. Fawcett, 1989.

6. Fritz, Robert. Your Life As Art. Newfane Press, 2003.

7. Itten, Johan. The Art of Color: The Subjective Experience and Objective Rationale of Color. Van Nostrand Reinhold, 1966.

8. Lamott, Ann. Bird by Bird: Some Instructions on Writing and Life Anchor Books, 1995.

9. May, Rollo. The Courage to Create. Norton, 2004.

10. Theroux, Alexander. The Primary Colors: Three Essays. Henry Holt, 1994.

11. Warren, Rick. The PurposeDriven Life. Zondervan, 2002.

LOOK FOR OUR
ART4HEALING® WORKSHOPS ONLINE

Visit us online at www.art4healing.org and join our Art4Healing®
Community where you can post photos of your paintings and
share about your experiences with Art4Healing®.

47973465R00048

Made in the USA
San Bernardino, CA
13 April 2017